Beavers

By Moira Rose Donohue

Children's Press®

An Imprint of Scholastic Inc.

Content Consultants
Carrie Pratt, M.Sc.
Curator, North America and Polar Frontier, Columbus Zoo and Aquarium
Nikki Smith
Assistant Curator, North America and Polar Frontier
Columbus Zoo and Aquarium

Library of Congress Cataloging-in-Publication Data

Names: Donohue, Moira Rose, author.
Title: Beavers/By Moira Rose Donohue.
Other titles: Nature's children (New York, N.Y.)
Description: New York, NY: Children's Press, An Imprint of Scholastic Inc., 2018. | Series: Nature's children |
Includes bibliographical references and index.
Identifiers: LCCN 2017058824| ISBN 9780531192634 (library binding) |
ISBN 9780531137567 (pbk.)
Subjects: LCSH: Beavers—Juvenile literature.
Classification: LCC QL737.R632 D66 2018 | DDC 599.37—dc23
LC record available at https://lccn.loc.gov/2017058824

Design by Anna Tunick Tabachnik

Creative Direction: Judith E. Christ for Scholastic

Produced by Spooky Cheetah Press

Printed in North Mankato, MN, USA 113

SCHOLASTIC, CHILDREN'S PRESS, NATURE'S CHILDREN™, and associated logos
are trademarks and/or registered trademarks of Scholastic Inc.

1 2 3 4 5 6 7 8 9 10 R 28 27 26 25 24 23 22 21 20 19

Scholastic Inc., 557 Broadway, New York, NY 10012.

Photographs ©: cover: Danita Delimont/Getty Images; 1: Musat/iStockphoto; 4 leaf silo and throughout: stockgraphicdesigns.com;4 top: Jim McMahon/Mapman ®; 5 child silo: All-Silhouettes.com; 5 beaver silo: Irina Iarovaia/Dreamstime; 5 bottom: Thomas Lazar/NPL/Minden Pictures; 6 beaver silo and throughout: lantapix/Shutterstock; 7: stanley45/iStockphoto; 8: Konrad Wothe/Minden Pictures; 11: Jody Ann/Shutterstock; 12: Thomas & Pat Leeson/Science Source; 15: John Webster/Getty Images; 16: Jim Brandenburg/Minden Pictures; 19 background: Michael Francis Photo/age fotostock; 19 inset: De Agostini Picture Library/Getty Images; 20 top left: Bernard Jaubert/Getty Images; 20 top right: Christy Davies/EyeEm/Getty Images; 20 bottom left: Chris002/Shutterstock; 20 bottom right: Yuliia Podusova/Shutterstock; 23: Yva Momatiuk & John Eastcott/Minden Pictures; 25: Rosanne Tackaberry/Alamy Images; 26: Robert McGouey/Wildlife/Alamy Images; 29: Thomas & Pat Leeson/Science Source; 30: Robert McGouey/Wildlife/Alamy Images; 33: Mark Mauno/Flickr; 34: Michael Durham/Minden Pictures; 37: Chris Howes/Wild Places Photography/Alamy Images; 38: Brad McGinley Photography/Getty Images; 41: Derek Davis/Portland Press Herald/Getty Images; 42 bottom: MediaProduction/Getty Images; 42 center: Joel Sartore/Getty Images; 42 top: Jody Ann/Shutterstock; 43 right: legna69/iStockphoto; 43 left: Joel Sartore, National Geographic Photo Ark/Getty Images.

Table of Contents

Fact File: Beavers

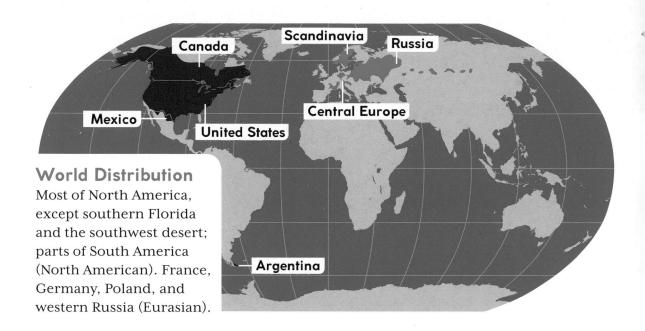

Canada

Scandinavia

Russia

Mexico

Central Europe

United States

Argentina

World Distribution

Most of North America, except southern Florida and the southwest desert; parts of South America (North American). France, Germany, Poland, and western Russia (Eurasian).

Habitat
Freshwater lakes, ponds, and streams

Habits
Mostly active at night; the sound of running water triggers them to build dams

Diet
Dine exclusively on twigs, the underside of tree bark, and water plants

Distinctive Features
Long front teeth; flat, scaly paddle-shaped tail

Fast Fact
The beaver is the national symbol of Canada.

Average Size

4 ft. 6 in.
(1.4 m)

Human (age 10)

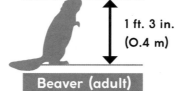

1 ft. 3 in.
(0.4 m)

Beaver (adult)

Classification

CLASS
Mammalia
(mammals)

ORDER
Rodentia
(rodents)

FAMILY
Castoridae
(beavers)

GENUS
Castor
(beavers)

SPECIES
- *Castor canadensis*
  (North American)
- *Castor fiber*
  (Eurasian)

◀ Beavers can stand
on ice, as shown, or
swim under it!

CHAPTER 1

The Busy Beaver

Chomp. Chomp. Craaaack! A beaver has chewed through the base of a tree near the riverbank. It **gnaws** through the log to make smaller pieces. Then the beaver clamps its teeth around one of the pieces and drags it into the river. It swims with the small log in its mouth to the dam it is building. The dam will hold back the river to form a new pond. That's where the beaver and its family will later make a home.

A beaver dam can turn a desert into a garden. It can create **wetlands** where there were none. Because wetlands benefit other animals, like water birds, beavers are a **keystone**, or important, **species**.

There are two species of beavers: the North American and the Eurasian. Today the North American beaver lives in most parts of the United States and Canada. A few North American beavers can be found in South America and Scandinavia because they were introduced to these areas by humans.

▶ A beaver chomps on a tree alone, so others aren't hurt when it falls.

Fast Fact

Beavers can hold their breath for up to 15 minutes.

Life in the Pond

Beavers are **semi-aquatic** animals. They spend most of their time in freshwater lakes, streams, and ponds. They even build their homes in the water.

These animals are excellent swimmers. Their back feet are webbed like a duck's, so they can paddle through the water. Beavers also have ear flaps that close when the animal dives into deep water. And they have an extra pair of see-through eyelids. These eyelids act like goggles when the beaver swims. Though beavers can see underwater, they don't have good eyesight.

The beaver's furry coat is also designed for aquatic life. It has two layers. The fur closest to the beaver's skin is thick and short. It traps air close to the beaver's body. This keeps the animal warm in the chilly water. On top is a layer of long, coarse guard hairs. Water slides right off.

◀ Beavers swim about 5 miles (8 kilometers) per hour.

9

Built to Build

The beaver is a type of **mammal** called a **rodent**. Rodents, such as mice and hamsters, have special front teeth that they use to gnaw on hard things. Beavers are the second-largest rodent in the world. Only the capybara, which lives in South America, is bigger. An adult beaver weighs between 24 and 65 pounds (10.9 and 29.5 kilograms). It can grow to almost 4 feet (1.2 meters) long, including its tail. Like many rodents, beavers are **nocturnal**. They work mostly at night.

Beavers' bodies are not only suited for life in the water. These mammals have certain traits that make them master builders, too. Their front paws have five flexible fingers. They are perfect for scooping up muck from the bottom of a pond to seal their dams. Beavers have claws on both their front and back feet for digging tunnels and canals.

Fast Fact
Though beavers have poor eyesight, their other senses are sharp.

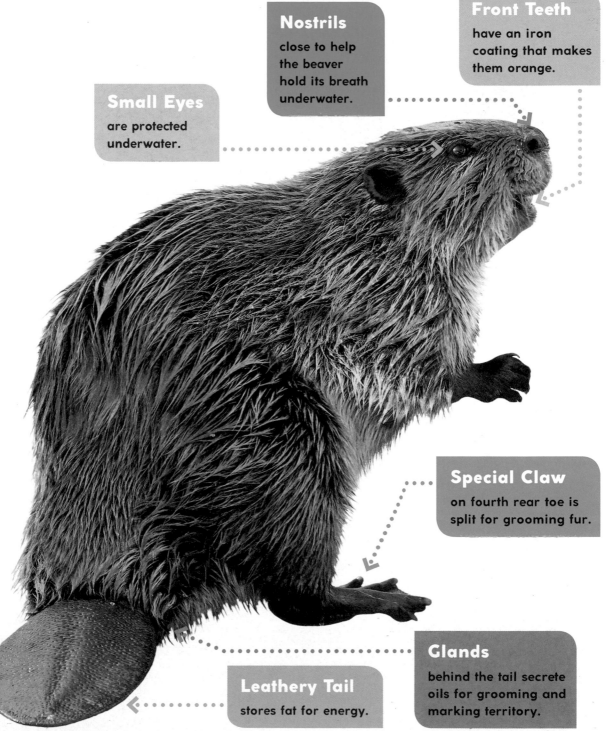

Nostrils
close to help the beaver hold its breath underwater.

Front Teeth
have an iron coating that makes them orange.

Small Eyes
are protected underwater.

Special Claw
on fourth rear toe is split for grooming fur.

Leathery Tail
stores fat for energy.

Glands
behind the tail secrete oils for grooming and marking territory.

The Tale of the Tail

SPLAT! That's the sound a beaver makes when it slaps its tail on the surface of the water. This loud splash is meant to scare away **predators** like coyotes, wolves, and bears. A tail smack can also be a warning to other beavers in the area. It sends a message that danger lurks nearby.

A beaver's distinctive tail is flat and shaped like a paddle. It can measure up to 8 inches (20.3 centimeters) wide and 1 ft. (0.3 m) long. It is covered with leathery, almost scaly, skin.

In the water, the beaver's tail helps it steer. On land, the beaver uses its tail for balance when it stands on its hind legs. And as the beaver drags its tail over the surface of the dam, it smooths out wet mud. As handy as the beaver's tail is, there's one thing it's not used for. A beaver does not slap its tail to pat down the mud.

◀ The sound of a beaver's tail slap can be heard more than a half mile (1 km) away.

CHAPTER 2

Nature's Engineers

Humans build houses, canals, and dams. Beavers do, too. Beavers are second only to humans in their ability to **adapt**, or change, their **environment**.

When a beaver searches for a place to live, it looks for deep water where it can build an underwater pantry. The beaver digs an area at the bottom of the pond to store food—twigs and branches—for the winter. That allows the animal to grab a snack without going outside in the cold. The water must be deep enough that it doesn't freeze solid in cold weather and cut off the beaver's food supply.

What if a beaver can't find a pond or lake that is deep enough? Well, that's no problem! The animal finds a stream or river. Then it starts to build a dam to hold back the running water. It helps that beavers have a sort of "sixth sense." The sound of trickling water automatically makes them start building a dam to stop the flow!

▶ In 1950, beavers were dropped into Idaho (*pictured*) by parachute.

Fast Fact
Beaver dams help
remove pollutants
from the water.

Natural Lumberjacks

To make a dam, a beaver starts by chopping down trees.
It can't hold an axe, so it uses its strong teeth to chip away
at a tree trunk. The beaver keeps working until the trunk
is attached by only a narrow point, and then ... Look out!
The beaver scurries out of the way as the tree finally falls.

Next, the beaver chews off the smaller branches. Then
it nibbles through the log to cut it into smaller pieces.

The beaver lays the logs on the bottom of the stream,
against the **current**. If the current is strong, the beaver
anchors logs with one end in the mud and the other end
sticking out at an angle. Then it piles branches, logs,
stones, and twigs between the anchor logs. Finally, the
beaver seals the dam with mud. The part of the dam we
see is just the top. Most of the structure is underwater!

◀ Beavers can eat
underwater without
choking.

Welcome to the Lodge

Beavers are not only engineers. They are also architects. They design their own homes, called lodges. They build their lodges in the ponds created by their dams.

From outside, a beaver lodge may look like just a heap of tangled sticks. But it's not. Inside the lodge is a large room that is 6 to 7 ft. (1.8 to 2.1 m) wide and 2 ft. (0.6 m) high. A grown man could lie down in it. The lodge must be big enough to fit a beaver's entire family. A beaver family, called a **colony**, may have 20 members.

The floor is built on piles of sticks so it's higher than the water level and stays dry. The beaver covers the floor with wood chips or dry grass. A vent, or hole, in the top of the lodge lets stale air escape. The only way to get inside a beaver lodge is underwater. A lodge has at least two tunnels underneath it that open up into the dry floor. These hidden entrances and exits keep the animals safe.

▶ A lodge looks like a pile of sticks—but it has a room and tunnels inside!

Linden Tree

Beavers strip the smooth bark off linden trees.

Maple Tree

▶ Beavers like to nibble on maple trees—especially the type called sugar maples.

Poplar Trees

▶ Poplar trees have a lot of starch in their bark, which is good for beavers.

Water Lilies

▶ In summer, beavers like to nibble on water lily roots.

Tasty Trees

Beavers don't eat the wood they chip away when cutting down trees. But they do chow down on other parts of the tree. They strip off the bark and nibble the softer layer just underneath it. Then they chew off the branches. They will store some of them for winter meals.

Beavers also munch on tender young twigs and leaves. Their favorite foods seem to be maples, linden, birch, and poplar trees. Beavers also eat water plants. They especially love water lilies.

Beavers gobble up at least 2 lb. (0.9 kg) of food a day. Digesting parts of trees isn't easy. Beavers digest their food twice. First they eat it and then poop out soft, green pellets. Then they munch the pellets and fully digest the softened wood.

◀ Beavers eat bark, leaves, and roots from these trees and water plants.

Fast Fact
April 7 is International Beaver Day.

Timber!

A colony of beavers is made up of a mother, father, and all of their children under the age of two. That many beavers need a lot of trees for food and building—200 to 300 trees a year! Luckily, a beaver can fell a small tree in 10 to 15 minutes. That's because the front side of the beaver's iron-coated teeth is extra strong.

Like other rodents, the beaver's front teeth never stop growing. But frequent gnawing through trees keeps them from getting too long. Beavers also grind their teeth together to sharpen them.

Beavers use their strong teeth to carry logs in their mouths to their building sites. They can haul logs that weigh as much as they do. A special lip behind the front teeth seals the beaver's mouth shut. That way, the beaver doesn't swallow water when it swims with logs in its mouth.

▶ The ends of beavers teeth are straight and knife-edge sharp.

CHAPTER 3

Life in the Colony

It's late spring in the beaver pond.

Yellow and white flowers decorate the bank and bright green leaves sparkle above. A two-year-old male beaver is nudged out of the lodge by its parents. It's time to find a pond of his own. As the beaver searches for a new pond, it checks for scent mounds.

Beavers use scent mounds to mark their **territory** and say: *This pond is taken!* They scratch up mud and make piles near their ponds. Then they squirt smelly oils from **glands**, or pouches, under their tails. One oil is called castoreum. Beavers also comb this oil through their fur to make it waterproof. At one time, people used castoreum for medicines, food flavorings, and perfumes.

Beavers have a strong sense of smell. They can recognize the scent of a relative. But if a beaver sniffs a new smell on a mound, the animal quickly moves on.

▶ Beaver oils actually smell good to humans.

Fast Fact
A lodge built into
a pond bank is
called a den.

Finding a Mate

The young male also keeps a lookout for a female. If he finds one, he will try to swim with her for a while. They may wrestle for fun in the water. They might even rub noses. That's the beaver form of a kiss.

If the female is interested in the young male, she will join him on his quest to find a new pond. And if they can't find a pond, they will build a dam to make one. Then the newlyweds will construct a lodge together. But they must hurry. They need to stockpile food in the underwater pantry before winter comes.

The beavers will stay together for life. They mate in the middle of winter. Three and a half months later, in May or June, the female gives birth to babies, called kits. Beavers have kits only once a year.

◄ A male and female beaver may wrestle and play when choosing a mate.

Here Come the Kits!

Just before the babies are due, the female beaver makes a soft bed in the lodge. **Litters** can contain from one to eight kits. Newborns are about 9 in. (23 cm) long and weigh less than 1 lb. (0.5 kg). They have fluffy fur. And their front teeth are already long!

Kits can often swim within 24 hours of being born. But it isn't safe for them to go into the water alone, especially at night. A nighttime predator, like an owl, can scoop up a tiny kit.

As the kits grow, they wrestle with each other. Sometimes they stand on their hind legs and wiggle back and forth to get one another's attention. For eight weeks, the kits drink their mother's rich milk. By the time they are football-sized, they are ready to take the plunge out of the lodge to find their own food.

▶ Only sea lions have richer milk than female beavers.

Fast Fact
Some dams are
more than 600 ft.
(183 m) long.

Beaver School

Beaver colonies are **matriarchal**. That means the mother is in charge of the family. She knows that the kits have a lot to learn. That's why they stay with their parents for two years or more. One of the first things they learn is toilet training. They must leave the lodge through one of the underwater tunnels when they have to poop.

By the time the kits are a year old, the mother is assigning them chores. The young beavers must get clean wood chips for the floor. And they must help babysit when the next litter of kits arrives.

When they are about one-and-a-half years old, beavers learn how to build. They will help repair the lodge and dam so no water gets through. And they will keep the underwater tunnels clear. They may help build additions to the dam, too.

◄ It looks like these beaver kits are being taught by a parent.

CHAPTER 4

Bear or Beaver?

Imagine a beaver that weighs between 132 and 220 lb. (59.9 and 99.8 kg). It would weigh nearly as much as some black bears! That's how big an ancient **ancestor** of the beaver—the giant beaver—was.

The giant beaver's body was similar to today's beaver's, but much bigger. Its front teeth were 6 in. (15.2 cm) long. Unlike a modern beaver, the giant beaver's teeth had ridges on the outside. And the tips of the front teeth were rounded. The giant beaver had a long tailbone, like a modern beaver. However, scientists can't tell from skeletons what the giant beaver's tail looked like.

This massive rodent roamed North America more than a million years ago. **Fossils** have been found in the southeastern part of the United States. Scientists believe the giant beaver spent time in the area that is now Florida. It became **extinct** about 10,000 years ago.

▶ The giant beaver lived during the last ice age.

My Cousin's a Rat

There are two other animals with the name beaver: the Eurasian beaver and the mountain beaver. But only the Eurasian beaver is actually the same species as the North American beaver. It lives in France, Germany, Poland, and western Russia.

The mountain beaver isn't a beaver at all, nor is it closely related to beavers. This rodent is a champion digger and spends most of its life underground.

The North American beaver's closest non-beaver relative is actually the tiny kangaroo rat. Though they are related, the kangaroo rat does not have much in common with a beaver!

This long-tailed rodent measures only 3.5 to 5.5 in. (8.9 to 14 cm). Like the kangaroo, this rat has strong back legs. They enable this wee animal to leap up to 9 ft. (2.7 m) if danger is nearby. That's almost 20 times its own entire body length!

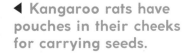

◄ Kangaroo rats have pouches in their cheeks for carrying seeds.

CHAPTER 5

Living with Beavers

Native Americans hunted beavers for their thick, warm under layer of fur. But they did not overdo it. They hunted only the animals they could use.

When European settlers arrived in North America, they found a large **population** of beavers. Europeans wanted their soft, warm fur for collars and coats. And later, men's hats made from beaver fur became popular. People throughout Europe and North America wanted one. Even President Abraham Lincoln had a beaver hat.

At first, settlers traded with the Native Americans— tools in exchange for beaver **pelts**. Then the settlers began trapping beavers on their own. Fur trapping became a big business. Soon beavers were overhunted. By the mid-1800s, the beaver population in North America had fallen from millions to only thousands.

▶ This hat is made from pressed beaver fur.

A Bigger Pond

Over time, people began to understand that beavers were important to the **ecosystem**. In the 1920s and 1930s, laws were passed to protect these animals. But that wasn't enough. So forest rangers moved some beavers to areas where there were none. Not every move was successful. Sometimes there were too many predators or the land didn't have the right trees to eat and the beavers died. But in many places, beavers made new homes and had families. Soon the beaver population returned. It's hard to measure the exact number of beavers in North America, but scientists think it could be in the millions again.

That's good news for the planet. Beaver dams build up clean water reserves and prevent soil **erosion**. They make new ponds, and new plants take root nearby. Sometimes an entirely new meadow is formed. And best of all, the dams create more wetlands. Wetlands help lots of animals. They are a **habitat** for water birds, and they provide homes for snakes and frogs.

◀ Beavers build dams on a curve if the current is strong.

Eager Beaver

Beavers are good for the environment, but occasionally they get in our way. Sometimes they build dams in areas that flood roads and buildings. Also, a young male beaver once cut down some of the famous Japanese cherry trees in Washington, D.C.

Covering tree trunks with wire mesh sometimes works to stop beavers. But often the beavers just find other trees to chop down nearby. Understanding a beaver's nature may be the key to resolving this problem. Some **conservationists** propose trying to attract beavers to build in certain areas by playing recordings of running water nearby. This may steer the beavers away from areas where they are not wanted. And scientists suggest building dirt hills drizzled with a beaver's scent oil. These may send a signal: *This area is occupied. Stay out!*

The more we know about nature's other engineers, the more we can appreciate them. And that gives us a better chance to happily share the planet with them.

▶ Here's an example of people and beavers managing to coexist!

North American Beaver Family Tree

Beavers are rodents, which are a type of mammal. Like other mammals, they are warm-blooded, have hair or fur, and usually have babies that are born live. Beavers even have five fingers. But unlike other mammals, rodents have front teeth that never stop growing. They use these teeth to gnaw through hard materials. This diagram shows how beavers are related to other rodents and non-rodents. The closer together two animals are on the tree, the more similar they are.

Gophers
medium-sized rodents that dig tunnels underground

Squirrels
common rodents found all over the world, except Australia

Note: Animal photos are not to scale.

Beavers
**medium-sized
semi-aquatic
rodents**

Kangaroo
Rats
**tiny rats that live
in tunnels in
the desert**

Rodents

Rabbits
**small mammals
related to beavers
that have soft fur
and long ears**

Ancestor
of all
Mammals

Words to Know

A .... **adapt** *(uh-DAPT)* to change because you are in a different situation

ancestor *(ANN-ses-tur)* a family member who lived long ago

C .... **colony** *(KAH-luh-nee)* a group of animals that live together

conservationists *(kahn-sur-VAY-shun-ists)* people who protect valuable things, especially forests, wildlife, or natural resources

current *(KUR-uhnt)* movement of water in a definite direction in a river or an ocean

E .... **ecosystem** *(EE-koh-sis-tuhm)* all the living things in a place and their relation to their environment

environment *(en-VYE-ruhn-muhnt)* the natural surroundings of living things

erosion *(i-ROH-shuhn)* the wearing away of something by water or wind

extinct *(ik-STINGKT)* no longer found alive

F .... **fossils** *(FAH-suhls)* bones, shells, or other traces of an animal or a plant from millions of years ago, preserved as rock

G .... **glands** *(GLANDZ)* organs in the body that produce or release natural chemicals

gnaws *(nawz)* bites or nibbles persistently

H .... **habitat** *(HAB-i-tat)* the place where an animal or a plant is usually found

K .... **keystone** *(KEE-stone)* something necessary or very important that other things depend on

L .... **litters** *(LIT-urs)* a group of animals born at the same time to one mother

M .... **mammal** *(MAM-uhl)* a warm-blooded animal that has hair or fur and usually gives birth to live babies; female mammals produce milk to feed their young

matriarchal *(may-tree-ARC-ul)* describes a family, group, or state ruled by a female

N .... **nocturnal** *(nahk-TUR-nuhl)* active at night

P .... **pelts** *(PELTZ)* animal skins with the hair or fur still on

population *(pahp-yuh-LAY-shuhn)* all members of a species living in a certain place

predators *(PRED-uh-tuhrz)* animals that live by hunting other animals for food

R .... **rodent** *(ROH-duhnt)* a mammal with large, sharp front teeth that are constantly growing and used for gnawing things

S .... **semi-aquatic** *(SEM-ee-uh-KWAT-ik)* living or growing partly on land and partly in water

species *(SPEE-sheez)* one of the groups into which animals and plants are divided; members of the same species can mate and have offspring

T .... **territory** *(TER-i-tor-ee)* an area that an animal or a group of animals uses and defends

W .... **wetlands** *(WET-landz)* land where there is a lot of moisture in the soil

Find Out More

BOOKS

- Brownell, M. Barbara. *Busy Beavers*. Washington, D.C.: National Geographic Society, 1988.
- Mara, Wil. *Beavers*. New York: Marshall Cavendish, 2008.
- Markel, Sandra, illustrations by Deborah Hocking. *Build, Beaver, Build! Life at the Longest Beaver Dam*. Minneapolis, MN: Millbrook Press, 2016.

WEB PAGES

- animaldiversity.org/accounts/Castor_canadensis/

  This Web site of the University of Michigan is authoritative and informative.

- www.nhptv.org/natureworks/beaver.htm

  The New Hampshire PBS Web site contains an excellent overview of the North American beaver.

- www.wdfw.wa.gov/living/beavers.html

  The State of Washington Department of Fish & Wildlife Web page has close-up photos and helpful diagrams.

Facts for Now

Visit this Scholastic Web site for more information on beavers:
www.factsfornow.scholastic.com Enter the keyword **Beavers**

Index

Index *(continued)*

About the Author

Moira Rose Donohue, a former attorney, is an animal lover who has written more than 25 books for children, including many about amazing animals. She lives with her dog, Petunia, in St. Petersburg, Florida. Find Moira at www.moirarosedonohue.net